Inconsequential Reflections

Sofia Pomeroy

Elpida Press
Kansas City

Special thanks to Brandon Pomeroy for formatting and editing.

Copyright © 2016 by Sofia Pomeroy

All rights reserved. No parts of this book may be used or reproduced in any matter whatsoever without written permission, except in the case of brief quotations embodied in critical articles or reviews.

Illustrations and cover design by Sofia Pomeroy

Published by Elpida Press
elpidapress@gmail.com
Elpidapress.org

ISBN: 978-0692757192
ISNB-10: 0692757198

For everyone with a story, aching to be heard.

Contents

Nature

Sonnet

Haiku Explains All

Reflections

Fear and Change

Nature

WINTER

An icy wind blows
across the frigid terrain,
and we walk faster.

The snow falls in large
clumps and will soon turn to ice,
so we slip and slide.

Time seems to have stopped,
but we must brave this icy
cold. It will soon end.

Gradually, it
becomes warmer. We throw on
less layers, smiling.

It's as if the sky
has granted us our one wish,
and that wish is spring.

SPRING

The earth seems to bloom
before our very eyes, and
we smile at the thought.

The skies open for
the first time since that cold, dark
place. It is springtime.

Time for pastels and
smiles that make it seem even
brighter than it is.

The day lasts longer,
giving us more time to do
whatever we want.

Eventually
the tulips wilt, and time slides
into the summer.

SUMMER

The birds begin to
chirp just as the sun rises,
and the day begins.

There's no stress at this
time of the year. Everyone
laughs quite joyfully.

Daylight lasts longer,
freeing us from the darkness
of the winter months.

How we spend our time
is up to us. We can do
whatever we want.

Slowly, things begin
to fade. And we remember
autumn is coming.

FALL

The leaves begin to
die and fall, changing to a
deep reddish-orange hue.

The happiness of
summer is gone, leaving a
melancholic state.

Autumn is the time.
Cozy sweaters and long hugs,
filling one with warmth.

What we feel is a
sadness for what we have lost,
glad for what we have.

Although autumn has
taken us from summer, it
has brought us back home.

CONTINUATION

The circle of life
continues with each passing
change of the season.

People come and go,
trees die, then come back to life,
truly a rebirth.

A rebirth, a sort
of natural renaissance
of people and plants.

A transformation
of the weather, and of our
own very beings.

The progression of
time and of people who will
continue to change.

CHANGE

The seasons change, but
we stay the same, even though
we try to improve.

For the world to be
a better place, the people
have to get along.

Fighting and putting
up walls won't help anything.
As one, we must try.

Try to stand up for
what we believe in, while we
bring people closer.

Closer so we can
all get along and go on
loving each other.

STRESS

Stress is a major
problem that seems to engulf
your very being.

It can eat you up
until you're nonfunctional
as a real person.

The key is to take
a step back. Don't let the stress
fully consume you.

Life is hard sometimes.
That's a common fact. But you
Must take charge of it.

And at the day's end,
all that's important is your
quality of life.

Sonnet

TOGETHER

With arms embraced around him, she's content.
While in his presence, the stars are aligned.
Laughing with him is as if heaven sent.
If only they'd always be intertwined.

Her giggle was a gift; he loved her smiles.
He longed for many quiet days with her.
He loved the way she wore messy hairstyles.
With her he was never an amateur.

Their eyes latched on to each other and glowed.
He only hoped she'd never look away.
Like a river, their love has always flowed.
She'll still be in love when her hair turns grey.

Under the moon, their eyes will always shine,
And he'll fight for the right to say, "she's mine."

AIRBORNE

High up in the clouds, you forget your strife.
You look down. All is insignificant.
From way up here, you think about your life,
And how it really is magnificent.

All that really matters is here and now.
Above the clouds you can figure things out.
Or, if you'd rather, you could just say "Ciao."
Or you could truly ponder your life's route.

From a plane, all life's dilemmas are shown.
Making you in complete control of you.
When you land, you can make your life your own,
And do the things you really want to do.

You get on the plane clueless and alone,
And exit thinking of how much you've grown.

FRENCH RIVIERA

As I'm walking through these beautiful streets,
Smiling, I'm grateful for this life I lead.
I really don't have that many defeats,
And I'm really not overcome with greed.

Les rues de France sont très belle et très calme.
The French accent is sophisticated,
And surprisingly complex, like my palm.
This trip to France has been much awaited.

Looking out to sea on the coast of Nice,
I look to the Mediterranean.
My worries and other harmful thoughts cease,
And I see a cute Pomeranian.

My fears dissipate as I look to the sea,
Yet I wonder what will become of me.

A LITTLE INSIGHT

Sitting over an iced cup of coffee,
I watch the hectic, busy world go by.
No one is paying attention to me,
But it's nice to have some people nearby.

I've always been the watcher, not the watched.
I just sit back, not at all affected.
Because of this, my life's never been botched,
And I've never felt neglected.

I take a small sip as they laugh and smile
And instead of jealous, I'm quite grateful.
Grateful for my life, which will last a while.
Full of thanks for a life that's not hateful.

I wonder why I'm not in the spotlight,
But remember that my life is still bright.

YOUTH

Driving down the road at ungodly speeds,
And with the music turned all the way up,
This happiness is all I'll ever need.
Much more fulfilling than clothes and makeup.

I turn to my best friend and we both laugh.
This is what being young needs to feel like.
A life we could never choreograph.
A life that is both awake and dreamlike.

We speed through the hard parts of our short lives,
But trying to still live in the moment.
Trying to live while forgetting our strife.
To open our eyes and not be dormant.

When we're trying to figure ourselves out,
Remember to keep your mind free of doubt.

SOUNDLESS

In the quiet, I can hear myself think.
I become filled with ideas and thoughts.
The world and my mind, at last, are in sync.
In the silence my mind twists into knots.

It's here that I can discover myself.
Discover why I think the way I do.
All alone, it's easy to find yourself.
Think about what you know, and what you knew.

I come here to find out what's important.
Determine what I value in my life.
What I want and what is inadvertent.
Here I think about my personal strife.

The absence of noise opens up my mind.
Myself and the world become intertwined.

THE ARTS

As the paint flows across the blank picture,
My imagination explodes with art.
While I am completely free from stricture,
The paint cascades directly from my heart.

Writing, I say what I normally can't,
More eloquent on paper than in speech.
Here, I'm more peaceful than a bright green plant.
My words can be sour, or sweet as a peach.

Writing and painting help me to unwind,
Especially after a draining day.
A detox to which I am quite inclined.
These two hobbies can bring me no dismay.

Not exceptional in either of these,
But what is needed is not expertise.

Haiku Explains All

SUNDAY

Every Sunday
morning my dad and I go
to a coffee shop.

Iced coffee and a
chai, as it always has been.
We sit down and sip.

We talk about our
plans and aspirations, or
just what's going on.

Peaceful mornings like
this help me get back on track
to what's important.

As we leave, we feel
that we really gained something
from our little chat.

THE PLAN

Okay, here's the plan
for the rest of my life, just
thought that you should know.

Graduate high school
in the top ten percent of
my large senior class.

Go to college at
a small liberal arts school
with outstanding grades.

Attend medical
school at KU, then finish
my residency.

Eventually
I will become a trauma
surgeon. That's the plan.

DAD

Dad, thank you so much
for loving me when no one
else will. I'm grateful.

Thank you for teaching
me to work to my fullest
capabilities.

Thank you for never
letting me give up on what
I want in my life.

Thank you for making
me laugh at your stupid jokes
and your anecdotes.

And, Dad, most of all,
thank you for making me the
girl I am today.

MOM

Mom, thank you for all
that you've taught me throughout the
years of my short life.

Thank you for taking
me shopping when no one else
ever quite wants to.

Thank you for being
there for me when I really
need my mom's support.

Thank you for teaching
me how to be dignified,
though I don't want to.

Above all else, I'm
Grateful for the wisdom you
Have passed down to me.

FRIENDS

Walking around the
Plaza, catching each other
up on our bright lives.

She tells me a joke
and I remember why we
are such close-knit friends.

I recount to her
a funny story, and she
reacts perfectly.

It's great to have friends
that are a superb fit for
you. Then you're happy.

Friends can help when you're
Feeling down, knowing just how
To be by your side.

TRANSLUCENT

Sometimes in school I
feel invisible, like no
one ever sees me.

I walk through the halls
with my head down, trying not
to make eye contact.

It's just so crowded,
and most people are a good
foot taller than me.

They look right over
me as if I'm not even
there. I don't exist.

Drowning in people,
I make my way to the next
class, hopefully seen.

TRY

I could never have
expected school to be this
difficult for me.

I thought I would just
sail through my academic
years and be just fine.

That was how it was
supposed to work. I don't try
and yet I succeed.

And now I'm really
trying and I don't feel like
I'm quite succeeding.

But I'm learning to
push myself harder than I
could've imagined.

Reflections

HOSPITALS

I think it started when
I began to understand
what my dad was
always talking about.
I became
interested.
Interested
in what it meant
to be a
doctor.
To save lives
on a daily basis, making them
better than they were
before.
I began to love
hospitals.
I associated hospitals not with
death
but with
life.
With joy rather than

sorrow.
Whether they're
rushed in or
there for a follow-up,
all patients are the same.
And should be treated the same.
A hospital
is like a big family.
Everyone depends on each other
to get things done,
and everyone
knows each other.
When I finally
stand in an operating room
with a scalpel in my hand,
I will finally
be happy.
Everything I've ever wanted
will have
come true.
I just can't wait.

RELAX

Curled up
on the couch,
I finally relax
after an exhaustingly
boring day at work.
I've found through my
16 and a half years of living
that it's important to relax.
Without giving yourself time to unwind,
you just become more tense,
and you forget what's important.
When you relax, you think.
And thinking is about the best thing
you can do for yourself.
Think through your
thoughts and opinions,
open yourself up,
to discover
what's truly inside.

BALLET

Ballet used to be my thing,
you know,
if I wasn't at school,
I was at ballet.
I started
when I was three,
and through the years
made it up to level six.
Ballet was the only sport
I could do.
And yes,
it is a sport.
I was never good at any sports
involving a ball,
or that included me
having to run.
Ballet gave me the
slim, trim body
I've always aspired to have.
I was never amazing at ballet,
but I loved watching the older girls

and company dancers.
I was awed at how
graceful and lithe
they were,
and I wanted to be them.
But after a while
ballet didn't amaze me
as much as it used to.
I began to
focus on school and my studies.
I began to
dread the long hours
in the studio.
Eventually I was expected to attend class
six days a week.
It filled every extra hour I had.
So last year was
my final year
at ballet.
I still miss it sometimes,
but I know it's better this way.
I finally have time to
hang out with my friends and

to actually have time to do homework.
So I guess
it worked out in the end.

SUMMER HAZE

I finally understand
why they call it
the "summer haze."
Winter is so sharp;
every moment feels
stagnant.
Every second is clear.
But summer,
summer rushes by
without a trace.
Seconds are indistinguishable from minutes.
Days no different than weeks.
Sitting outside during the summer
even feels hazy.
It's so loud in the summer too.
Every creature
decides to sing their song
on days like these.
The people blast their playlists,
the birds chirp at sunrise,
and the cicadas make that infuriating noise.

But in the winter,
every sound is crisp.
You can hear
a car going by
from your upstairs bedroom.
Time stalls in the
colder months.
It seems like it will
never end.
I assume that's why
people love summer.
Worries disappear, and
cares fade into the haze.
People lounge around outside
for a whole season.
Me, I'm more of a winter person.
Maybe I just like the cold, or
maybe I'm just not a relaxed enough person for
summer.
I'd much rather breathe in
the knife-like, cold air
instead of
the hot, muggy sort.

But I certainly understand why
people love to be
wrapped in the warm summer haze.

Fear and Change

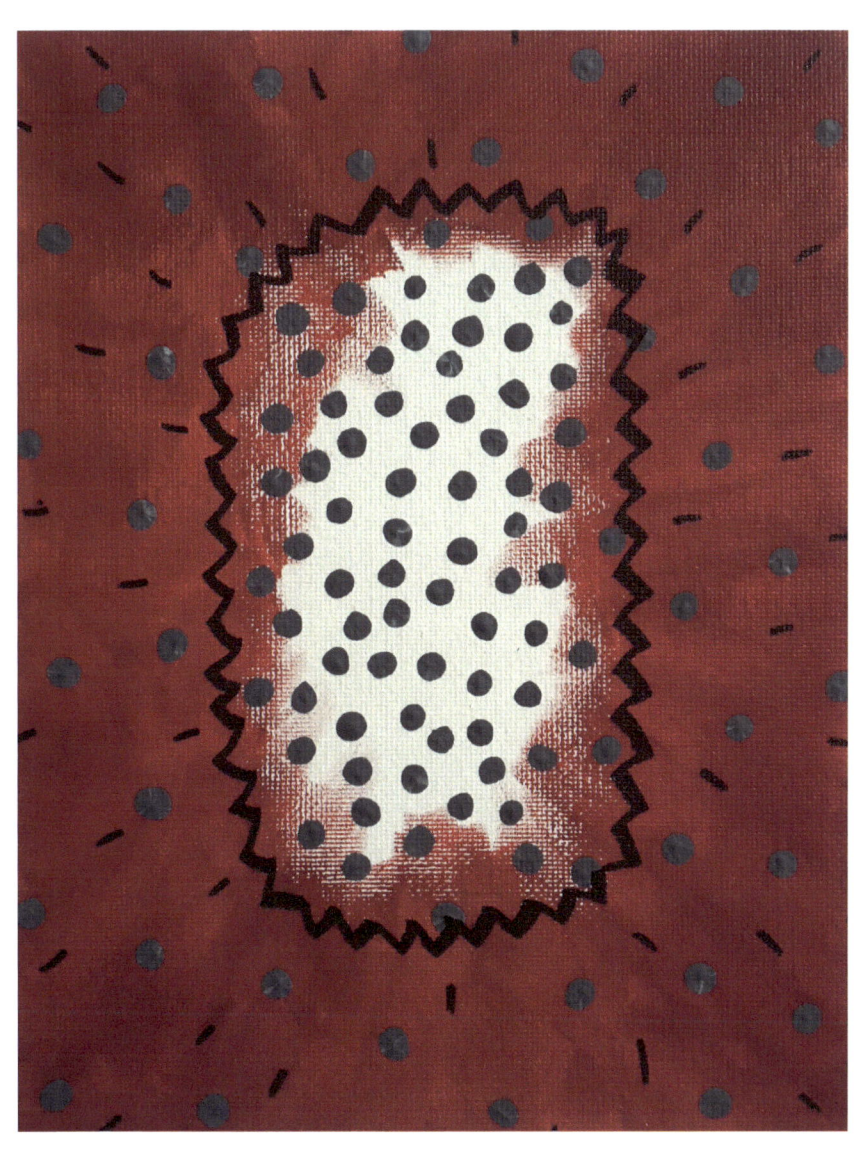

AGED

Sitting here
with my husband
at the ripe old age of 76,
I look back
on my blessed life.
I married him at 27,
just out of all those years of school,
and had our wedding in England.
Neither of us wanted kids,
so we settled in rainy Seattle
and I worked at a hospital there.
I think about
all the people I put back together,
and remember
the ones I lost.
I followed my dream
of becoming a trauma surgeon,
and it made me
the happiest I've ever been.
My husband
was a nurse at KU,

and we met
when I was in medical school.
Eventually,
he decided he wanted to become more
specialized,
so he went back to school.
and became a flight nurse.
We were perfect for each other.
We worked well
under stress
and difficulty.
We travelled all around the world together.
To Paris,
Rome,
London,
Sicily,
Amsterdam,
Stockholm.
I am truly blessed with this life.
I've seen every type of person.
And sitting here,
in my wooden rocking chair,
my heart is full.

CHANGE

The summer of my 16th year
my pastor said something
that really stuck.
She said,
"We can change this world."
WE can change this world.
We CAN change this world.
We can CHANGE this world.
We can change THIS world.
We can change this WORLD.
When the emphasis is put
on different words
the meaning changes.
This short phrase
followed me throughout my life.
It inspired me
to do what seemed
beyond my reach.
Whenever I was faced with an obstacle,
I thought,
"We can change this world."

Whenever I disagreed with someone,
I thought,
"We can change this world."
And really,
who's to say we can't?
Why can't we change this world?
What's stopping us?
How can we reach our fullest potential?
All that we need is an idea.
One idea,
one thought,
one dream
to push us farther that we thought possible.
Just one common goal and
we can change this world.
These thoughts shaped my thinking
my entire life.
These words reminded me to
never give up.
This small phrase helped me to
never let go of my dreams,
because
we can change this world.

GONE

I never thought I would
outlive my parents.
It seems impossible
and slightly cliché,
but I always assumed they would
live forever.
Untouched by fate.
I never planned for it,
because I assumed
it would never happen.
Like when it was time for them to go,
I thought we would all
magically cease to exist.
Which is why I was surprised when
they were gone.
Both of them.
I was suddenly
alone
and without guidance.
I was expected to
proceed as usual.

But time slowed down.
Every second was parent-less.
I wondered how
such a large percent of the population
goes on
without parents.
I suddenly had no one that would
listen to my fiery rants and
my prepared soliloquies.
No one that would
understand me in a way that
no one else does or ever will.
Eventually
I learned how to live without them.
I learned how to
carry on about my day
as if nothing is horrifically awry.
I learned to
let go of the past
while still remembering it.
The one thing parents can never teach you
is how to let them go.

FIN

Now I sit on my deck
in my wooden rocking chair
and I am content.
I'm proud of all the choices I made
throughout my life.
I made a myriad of mistakes
and had a plethora of positive outcomes.
My life's dreams have been
fulfilled
and for that I'm glad.
I just hope everyone else's life
is as blessed as mine.

This last haiku doesn't quite fit into any one section, but I insist on sharing it. It came to me in Arles, France. We had been to the same patisserie three days in a row, and I was excited to try a triple-layered chocolate cake. We were sitting on the balcony outside our room on my $5/12^{th}$ birthday when it suddenly began to rain.

Rain on my small cake.
Not how you keep a cake moist!
Overly moistened.

What a beautiful mess life is.

-Sofia

Acknowledgments

I would like to thank the following (groups of) people for their unwavering support towards the reaching of my goals:

Shawnee Mission East High School, for educating me and aiding in the realization of who I strive to be; Peace Christian Church, for helping to shape me, spiritually and emotionally; my friends, for keeping me young, and never failing to believe in what I can do; Brandon Pomeroy, for listening to my long-winded rants, and for always understanding me, even when no one else does; Lucie Pomeroy, for teaching me what it takes to be a strong-willed young woman; and Jackson Pomeroy, for being my built-in best friend.

About Elpida Press

In our busy lives, when we are only able to see things superficially and quickly, when information comes in headlines and sarcastic quotes, when everything seems fragmented and temporary, and when our actions are motivated by fear rather than hope, Elpida Press provides an alternative. A non-profit publishing company unsatisfied with the status quo, we are committed to love and reconciliation. We are on the lookout for skilled artists and writers to work with. As a non-profit we are also dependent on your kind donations. Every little bit helps as we strive to be part of the solution, carefully mending and repairing what has been nearly torn apart.

Please visit our website and follow us on Facebook.

Elpidapress.org
Facebook.com/elpidapress

Also from **Elpida Press**

Nearly as far away as you can imagine, in a remote and dusty West African town, there is a school that defies the odds. In a predominantly Muslim country, students are studying the Bible. Where most kids struggle to read, children are being prepared for high school and beyond. *Grace Upon Grace* tells the story of Ibrahima Kodio who has created a special place whose effects continue to ripple through the students, the teachers, the families, and through all who support and pray for them.

Available now at Elpidapress.org and Amazon.com

Also from **Elpida Press**

"A spiritually thought provoking and thoroughly engaging novel."
-Newell Williams, President of Brite Divinity School at TCU

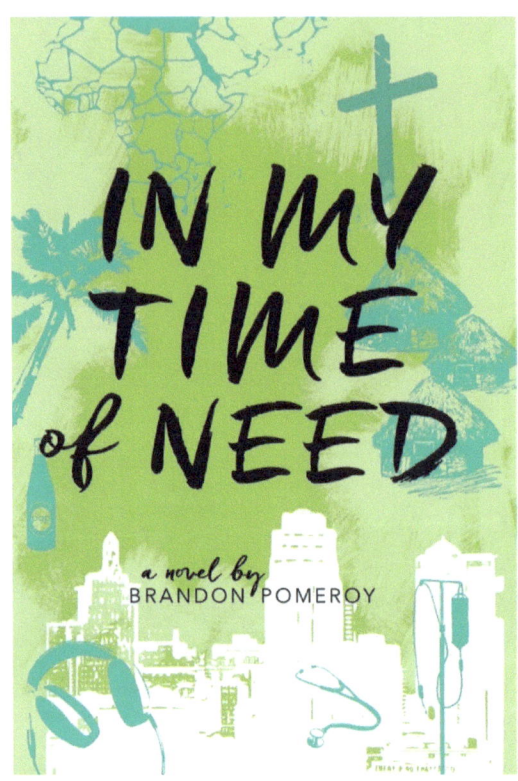

Brandon Pomeroy's novel, *In My Time of Need*, is an unconventional love story that takes the reader from Kansas City to Central America and East Africa. Filled with grace and humor, it is a spiritual journey that is as universal as it is meaningful.

Available now at Elpidapress.org and Amazon.com